MOMENTS
WITH
CHAPLIN

MOMENTS
WITH
CHAPLIN

Lillian Ross

DODD, MEAD & COMPANY
NEW YORK

Copyright © 1978, 1980 by Lillian Ross
All rights reserved
No part of this book may be reproduced in any form
without permission in writing from the publisher
Printed in the United States of America

1   2   3   4   5   6   7   8   9   10

The text of this book appeared
originally in *The New Yorker*

ISBN: 0-396-07829-X
Library of Congress Catalog Card Number: 80-80828

MOMENTS
WITH
CHAPLIN

CHARLIE CHAPLIN

was the first international movie star. He was also the first movie figure to be widely regarded as a genius. Through all the decades since Chaplin's arrival in Hollywood in the early years of motion-picture history; through all the changes and developments that have taken place in the industry with the advent of sound, color, new cameras, new dollies, the wide screen, stereophonic sound, big studios, no studios, big budgets, little budgets, big and rich producers, little and poor producers, big-star pictures, no-star pictures, big agents, the bankers in the background, the tie-ins with books, the tie-ins with records; through the rise of the director, the rise of the movie writer, the rise of movie-theory jargon, the rise of intellectuals as custodians of the art of "film," the rise of college courses in "film," the rise of the lecture circuit on "film," the rise in the power of the stars, and the superpower of the superstars; through the strain to compete with television, the strain to coöperate with television; and through the countless technological advances—through everything, Charlie Chaplin has persisted as a gigantic, incomparable figure. His pictures have by now been seen by billions of people all over the world. For many years, Chaplin's life, like that of many movie stars, was disrupted, or at least thrown into confusion, by publicity of one kind or another, but at the age of fifty-four he married Oona O'Neill, the daughter of Eugene O'Neill, and with her he settled down into a period of astonishing serenity, which lasted as long as he lived. I first met the Chaplins in Hollywood, at a party, in 1948, when they were living in Beverly Hills with the first two of their eight children, and I continued to see them from time to time over the subsequent years. Their home always served as a refuge from the Hollywood frenzy, a very nice refuge—with a tennis court, a pool, and regular Sunday outdoor teas—which they shared graciously with other refugees of all kinds, both foreign and domestic. It was great fun for me, for one thing, to talk in a relaxed way with guests like Jean Renoir, James Agee, and Carol Matthau in that setting. For another thing, I spent some pleasant hours on the Chaplins' tennis court, playing with (or against) Chaplin, who always played to win.

A number of moments from Chaplin's life remain fixed in my memory. There was a moment in 1950 when I found Chaplin and Oona in their kitchen fussing over a leg of lamb that they were roasting, while a couple of small children stood by watching. Food was always important to Chaplin, because, as he used to explain, he had been so often deprived of it when he was a child. On this day, he was in charge of the oven, a chef's big white apron tied around his waist, a big spoon in his left hand, and he was giving the lamb his full concentration, with a Charlie Chaplin pursing of the lips, a

Charlie Chaplin

Charlie Chaplin frown, a Charlie Chaplin raising of the spoon at his wide-eyed, frozen onlookers, to keep them at their distance.

"It's done now," he reported, rather nervously. "It's just right. Tender and succulent."

"Charlie did the basting while I fed the baby," his wife said.

"I baste and baste," Chaplin said to me, with authority. "Baste and baste and baste."

In Hollywood, Chaplin was restless whenever he was not working on a movie, and there were often long stretches between movies. In 1950, on a chilly, damp evening during one of these periods, I watched Chaplin take a hand in directing the James Barrie play "What Every Woman Knows," at the Circle, Hollywood's leading noncommercial theatre. The play was starring Ruth Conte and Sydney Chaplin, Charlie Chaplin's second son (by an earlier marriage, to Lita Grey), who was then twenty-four. (Charles Chaplin, Jr., Sydney's older brother by the same marriage, and the first of Chaplin's children, died in 1968 at the age of forty-two.) The Circle had practically no money, and the regard in which it was held, particularly by actors and actresses in pictures, was quite out of proportion to its financial standing. Many movie people contributed their talents without pay. One was Shelley Winters, who was directing the play "Thunder Rock," by Robert Ardrey. Another was Chaplin. Everybody associated with the Circle was serious about acting and about the theatre. The Circle's manager, Jerry Epstein, was an energetic, dedicated, good-natured young man from Brooklyn who lived in an apartment behind the theatre, as did Sydney Chaplin. Epstein eventually worked with Charlie Chaplin as an all-around assistant on "Limelight," the assistant producer of "A King in New York," and the producer of "A Countess from Hong Kong," the last three movies that Chaplin made. Sydney Chaplin became, and still is, a movie actor. But in 1950 the Circle was their life. The theatre was a small, round room, seating a hundred and fifty people at most, in a dank, dilapidated building in the heart of Hollywood. The audience was ranged in tiers around a vacant space about the size of the back seat of a station wagon. The actors performed in this area. The management of the Circle always cautioned its audience to come on time. "You come late and you find yourself in the play," Jerry Epstein told me.

Sydney Chaplin was on the Circle's board of directors, along with Epstein and an actor named William Schallert. "I love the Circle, except that it's lousy to wake up and *be* here," Sydney Chaplin said to me the evening I watched his father in action at the theatre.

"It's the only place in town where you can *act*," Schallert said solemnly.

"We couldn't get Charlie Chaplin for any amount of *money*," Epstein said. "He *likes* to come down and direct."

Epstein took a broom and started sweeping out the theatre to prepare it for the director. A young girl wearing ballet slippers wandered in and asked him when "Thunder Rock" would open. Epstein said he didn't know. Shelley Winters had been rehearsing it for four months, he said, so it ought to open soon. "Shell is trying to give it some kind of existentialist touch," he said. Then he turned to Sydney Chaplin and asked, "You nervous, Sydney?"

"I'm beat," Sydney said. "I was up till seven this morning painting and papering this joint."

Chaplin arrived at about eight o'clock, dressed for the chilly, damp evening in a salt-and-pepper tweed suit over a sweater.

"Hello, Papa," Sydney said.

"Where's the cast?" Chaplin asked crisply.

Chaplin

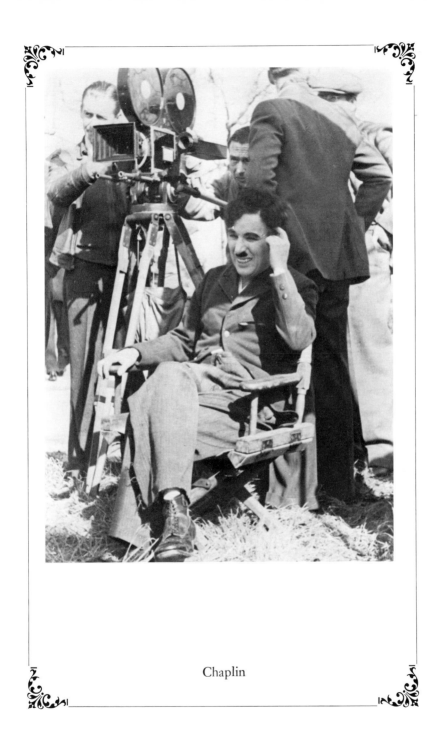

Chaplin

Chaplin

Epstein and Schallert and Sydney Chaplin immediately called the cast and various theatre aides and told them to take their stations. Chaplin got to work at once. He started talking the moment the rehearsal got under way, with the actors playing the parts of a Scottish quarry owner and his two sons discussing the problems of the quarryman's spinster daughter, played by Ruth Conte.

"Don't let it get doleful!" Chaplin said. "Make it very warm. It's cold outside, but you get a glow, a warm glow."

He turned to Schallert, who, in addition to being the nominal director, was playing the elder son, and said, "Keep moving. Do something with your hands."

Chaplin took a seat in the front row, hunched his shoulders, and frowned at his cast. "All right, let's go, let's go," he said impatiently. "Keep it going. Keep it going, keep it going." To one of the two sons he said, "You bring it *down*. Keep it up. Keep it *up*."

He paused for a few moments, then addressed the whole cast. "This first part is everything," he said. "That's why I'm dwelling on this. You must not act. You . . . *must* . . . *not* . . . *act*. I must sharpen you here. No self-pity. Don't give the audience the impression that you've just read the script. It's phony now. We don't talk that way. Just state it. Don't make it weary. You're too young for that. Let's get away from acting. We don't want acting. We want reality. Give the audience the feeling that they're looking through the keyhole. This will be maudlin and sticky as hell if you act. The play is sentimental enough. Don't do it with broken hearts. Come on. If you get a tear in the voice, it's ruined. Come on, now. Come on."

After the actors had spoken a few more lines, he said, "Get the feeling of embarrassment rather than self-pity. I like that. I like that. It's more noble. Get all the murkiness out of it now."

Chaplin slouched down in his seat, biting his thumbnail, and watched quietly for a while—until Sydney Chaplin came onstage, in the role of the ambitious young man who breaks into the family's home to read and study their books. Sydney took a book from a shelf and sat down to read it. Chaplin leaped to his feet, and, elbowing his son out of the chair, demonstrated how an interloper makes himself comfortable in someone else's house. He gave a small, Chaplinesque hiccup to show the way he made himself at home. "Get the drama in this, Sydney," Chaplin said, returning to his seat. "Get the drama. It's a situation. Make it clean."

Again, he hunched down in his seat. A moment later, he was back on his feet. "Sydney, for Christ's sake, get rid of that singsong. Get rid of those inflections. Just say the thing. You're not cheeky. You're never cheeky. You're indignant. They think you're a burglar, and, goddammit, you're not. You're a student."

Shortly afterward, he burst out laughing with what seemed to be pure pleasure. "Great humor!" he said as Sydney spoke with indignation instead of with cheekiness. "Charming," he went on. "Lovely humor. Lovely." He gave a little sigh of satisfaction.

The next moment, he was elbowing Sydney out of his place onstage again. "You must *think* rather than parrot the words," he said. "All right. All right. Don't lay an egg. Keep it going."

As the spinster daughter confronted the student, Chaplin said, "Don't break the thing between the two of you. You must get the nuance of this thing. This is somebody you're going to be very intimate with. It'll be so sweet. So sweet." Chaplin looked buoyant and happy, while Sydney chewed nervously on his lips.

"We must keep the choreography clean," Charlie Chaplin pleaded as the actors moved awkwardly around the small stage

16

Chaplin

Chaplin, 1925

area. He worked tirelessly on the choreography for a half hour or so, and then went back to rehearsing the first scene between Ruth Conte and Sydney.

"Sydney, say those lines as though you were saying them!" he cried. "Make it simple. Make it sincere. All this lousy singsong. I loathe that singsong. It hurts me."

He bounded around the stage incessantly—energetic, enthusiastic, fervent, and apparently tireless, as the actors and actresses began to wilt. He examined them from every angle. He looked closely into their faces. He stood on chairs and looked down at them. He knelt on the floor and looked up at them. At one point, he shoved one of the actors out of a chair. "May I sit here?" he said after he was sitting there. "I want to sit here for a while. I want to *feel* it."

After five hours of rehearsal, the cast was exhausted. Chaplin looked as fresh as he had at the beginning.

"Keep it simple!" he cried. "Too many gestures are creeping in. I don't like that. If the audience notices a gesture, you're gone. Gestures are not to be seen. And I'm a gesture man. It's hard for me to keep them down." As he spoke, he made a small, delicate gesture of restraint. "Thank God, I can see myself on the screen the next day," he added.

A little while later, he was showing the cast how to go on and off the stage. "I'm essentially an entrance-and-exit man," he said. "Good exits and good entrances. That's all theatre is. And punctuation. That's all it is."

When the rehearsal was over, Chaplin told the actors they would be very good on opening night.

They looked slightly revived. Jerry Epstein beamed. "You were wonderful tonight, Mr. Chaplin," he said. "Thank you very much."

Chaplin looked delighted, and ready to start all over again. "Keep it simple," he said briskly. "Keep it sincere. Now, what about some wheat cakes and coffee?"

It was almost three in the morning. With the cast and management of the Circle at his heels, he set off at a fast clip for an all-night beanery that could supply wheat cakes and coffee.

In September, 1952, Chaplin and his wife came to New York. They came by train, stopping in Chicago briefly en route. Chaplin's newly finished movie, "Limelight"—the last movie he made in this country—was scheduled to open shortly, and after that they were planning to sail on the Queen Elizabeth, with their children (there were four by then: Geraldine, Michael, Josephine, and Victoria), for Chaplin's first visit to London in twenty years, on what he thought was going to be a vacation. He did not yet know that on the ship he would be informed by the United States government that, as a British subject suspected of "left-wing leanings," he would not be welcome to return to the United States. When the Chaplins arrived in New York, they checked into the Sherry-Netherland, and Oona called me to ask if I wanted to go walking with Charlie around the city. "I can't go," Oona said. "He walked me for four hours in Chicago. I've got blisters on both heels."

The next morning at eleven, I went to pick Chaplin up at their suite.

"Walking around the city is a ritual with me," Chaplin told me as he ushered me in. "I love to walk all over New York. It's a bloody ritual with me."

Oona smiled and rubbed her feet.

Chaplin looked at her with unabashed affection and admiration. "She's a bloody Victorian," he said. "The only woman I know who carries *smelling* salts!"

Chaplin was dressed for the walk in an oxford-gray double-breasted suit, a white shirt with a black satin necktie, and gray socks and well-shined black shoes. His hair, pure white even then, was long, curling up at the back of his neck. His eyebrows, too, were pure white. His cheeks were pink. He was smiling, and was eager to get going. "This isn't too bad, now, is it?" he asked, waving a hand around the living room of the suite. "At least, it's light. At first, they took us to a dark-green room with red drapes. The gloomiest bloody place, with holes in the drapes. Can you imagine that? Holes in the drapes! We had to move. I like brightness. My brother and I were brought up in a dark hovel, and I'm not having any more of that—am I?" He smiled at his wife, and she smiled back.

Out on the sidewalk, Chaplin took a deep breath. "I like this kind of day for walking in the city," he said. "A sultry, Indian-summer September day. But do you know the best time for walking in the city? Two A.M. It's the best time. The city is chaste. Virginal. Two A.M. in the winter is the best, with everything looking frosty. The tops of the automobiles. Shiny. All those colors." He took another deep breath. "It's really hot today," he said. "Thank God I left my vest off."

We started out, walking south on Fifth Avenue. "There used to be a florist right here," Chaplin said at Fifty-eighth, looking puzzled. "His name was Schling. He was a philosopher. I could never pass by without his saying 'Come in here,' and he would stick a flower in my lapel. He was full of emotion. Very talkative. He always gave you a reason he liked to sell flowers." Chaplin laughed, and then arranged his face in that inimitable eager-to-please, self-abnegating, teeth-baring, lingering smile.

Not many people among the passers-by seemed to recognize Chaplin as we walked. He was smiling a bit to himself, as though he noticed that he wasn't being recognized, and got a kick out of it.

"The first time I came to New York from Hollywood, I

stopped traffic on Broadway," he told me when I remarked on the near-anonymity. "One of the newspapers had a big headline—'HE'S HERE!' That's all. The police chief, I remember, made me get off the train at a Hundred and Twenty-fifth Street to avoid the mobs. That was in 1916."

Chaplin was approached only a few times on this walk. He was approached first by a young woman carrying a paper shopping bag, who asked him to shake hands with her ten-year-old son, Paul. He shook hands with Paul. Then he was stopped by the wife of the film director Lewis Milestone, who asked him about his children. Chaplin told her that he had shown "City Lights" to them just before leaving California, and that they had all cried—had thought the movie was very, very sad. Then he met the actor Mel Ferrer, who yelled "Charlie!" They shook hands. "I was just watching you on television last night," Ferrer said, "One of your two-reelers. You in the ashcan—remember?"

"Yes, yes," Chaplin said, with his laugh. "You know, I haven't seen any of my pictures on television. We don't have a television set."

Ferrer asked him what he was doing in the city, and Chaplin said he had brought an advance print of "Limelight" with him to show at a few screenings before it opened. Ferrer said he wanted to see the picture, and observed that there was a world of difference between pictures made by Chaplin and those made by everybody else.

"I know—I use my own *dough*," Chaplin said, and he laughed again. "I woke up this morning, and I suddenly realized I had just spent a million dollars making the picture, and I said to myself, 'My God! What have I done?'" Mel Ferrer and I were treated to a quick reënactment by Chaplin, in pantomime, of Charlie Chaplin waking up to what he had done.

"Seems as if I'd been here forever," Chaplin said to me as

we continued our walk down Fifth Avenue. "You come along this avenue and you meet the world. In Hollywood, you walk for miles and you don't meet a single friend. Sometimes when I have a whole day here I walk a whole day. I just go along, and I discover places. I discovered Sweet's, the famous fish place, all by myself. Down near the Battery. To me, that's the romantic part of New York. Especially on Sunday. It's so quiet down there. So chaste. So clean. Nobody's around. You take any business center, there's something very romantic about it when it's inactive. So I went walking down there to the Battery by myself and saw this place with all the limousines parked outside. Dowagers stepping out of the limousines. Very respectable gentlemen. So I said to myself, 'This must be very good.' And I went in there and had myself a load of clams. I love clams. I used to go to Grand Central— to the Oyster Bar. I'd get a dozen clams, and all you'd want besides is the lemon. You'd get a dozen clams for eighty cents."

We walked along in silence for a few moments. Chaplin looked with interest at the other pedestrians.

"Every time I walk, I get a terrific exhilaration," he said. "Each new day is a day of promise. There are always parts of the city to explore. Always parts you haven't seen. The first time I saw Fifth Avenue was in 1910, when I first arrived in New York, from England, with Fred Karno's vaudeville troupe. I was very poor. I was the leading comedian in a sketch called 'The Wow Wows.' I wasn't getting much money, even though I was getting twenty-five dollars more than the others in the troupe. In those days, all the actors, in the summertime, used to go to Coney Island to work as waiters. I never did it, because I was getting more than the rest."

After we'd gone a couple of blocks, he continued, "On Fifth Avenue, they used to have those cafés out on the sidewalk. There was one very attractive Victorian place, with brass rails. I used to walk up and down in front of those cafés

Chaplin in "His New Job," 1915

Chaplin in "The Floorwalker," 1916

Chaplin in "Easy Street," 1917

Chaplin and Jackie Coogan in "The Kid," 1921

Chaplin and Georgia Hale in "The Gold Rush," 1925

Doing the Dance of the Dinner Rolls in
"The Gold Rush"

Chaplin and Virginia Cherrill in "City Lights," 1931

Chaplin in "Modern Times," 1936

looking at the people having their tea and their cakes. In those days, you didn't ever see women in pants. You wouldn't think of going on Fifth Avenue without a derby and a cane."

"Hi, Charlie!" a man in a business suit called out as he hurried by us.

"Oh, *hello!*" Chaplin called back, looking surprised and waving at the man.

"Isn't this lovely weather?" he asked me. "I feel absolutely marvellous. I'm supposed to get some clothes. And I need a haircut. So many things. You know, in 1910, when I first arrived in New York, it was just this kind of a day in September. Indian summer. Funny thing. We got off the boat and had our luggage sent to the theatre—to the Colonial Theatre, at Sixty-second and Broadway. The theatre is gone now. I can conduct you on a tour. Tell you all about New York in 1910 and in 1912. I've outlived it all."

Chaplin clasped his hands behind his back as we passed the Scribner Bookstore. "I used to haunt the secondhand-book shops in those days," he said. "I was pretty lonesome. It was the most terrible lonesomeness I've ever felt, that first year in New York. Anyway, the day I got off the boat in New York, I planted myself right in the middle of Broadway. I didn't know how to function at all. I had taken a streetcar, and I got off at Times Square. There were all those old brownstones, rooming houses, where English people looked for digs, all along there. I took a little back room, for three bucks a week. There used to be a saloon near where the Paramount Theatre is now. I later stayed in a room above the saloon. I was terribly ill there. For two days, I couldn't get out of bed. They used to have a magnificent free lunch. God, in those days! What an array! The pigs' knuckles! Ham sandwiches! Sauerkraut! Hot dogs! All free! Let's go over that way. To where the American Music Hall used to be. I played there with the Fred Karno troupe for six weeks in 1911. Near the corner of Eighth Avenue, on Forty-second Street. I like to go look at it. But let's not go on Forty-seventh or Forty-eighth Street. They're very sad streets."

We turned north again, and then walked west beside the Plaza Hotel.

"The Plaza was very new, very magnificent when I was first here," Chaplin said. "And the big thing then was Riverside Drive. That was the really posh place to live, in one of those mansions on Riverside Drive. There are so many streets I like, but I don't suppose we'll get to them today. Second Avenue. There was great vitality on Second Avenue when it had all those houses with little gardens."

When we reached Times Square, Chaplin stood in front of the Police Department information booth and looked around. He took some tortoise-shell-rimmed glasses out of his inside coat pocket and put them on.

"None of the houses or anything are left now," he said. "You know, I was very young when I lived here. Not yet twenty-two. I had my twenty-second birthday in St. Paul, Minnesota, with the Karno troupe. 'A Night in an English Music Hall,' the act we were doing then was called. Do you know what I used to do? I'd sit in a box in the theatre and interfere with everything—all the business going on on the stage. I'd disapprove, disrupt, make noise. In another act, 'A Night at a London Club,' I also played a drunk. The comedians in those days always played an older man. I remember going out to the West Coast and meeting Mack Sennett for the first time. He had seen me at the American Music Hall and thought I was a much older man. Offstage, at twenty-two, I looked about sixteen." Chaplin gave his laugh. "I'll never forget the time I got the message that Mack Sennett wanted me for Keystone. I was here in New York and got a message to come to the Longacre Building, where all the lawyers had their offices. My immediate thought was that rich relatives in America were trying to find me. I was so disappointed when I learned that Adam Kessel and Charles Bauman, who owned Keystone, wanted to tell me that what I was wanted for was the *movies*."

Forty-second Street. Chaplin headed for the Rialto Theatre, which was showing movies. " 'Bela Lugosi Meets a Brooklyn Gorilla.' " Chaplin read from the marquee. "This used to be *the* showplace," he said. "It was called the Victoria. Hammerstein's! The first Oscar Hammerstein himself used to stand on the curb outside here. You know, it was Willie Hammerstein, Oscar's son, who invented pie-throwing. The legend is that Mack Sennett invented it. But when the Karno company worked for Willie Hammerstein, he loved the act, and he gave us a bit of business for the act with the dour drunks." Chaplin lowered his voice a couple of octaves and, putting on a pompous manner, sang, "Hail, morn, smiling morn." He went on, "We had a boy in the box with me, and I used to knock him over. One day, Hammerstein said, 'Why don't you do it with a pie?' So we did. The goo of it. The laughter we got lasted two minutes, which was a long time. Willie Hammerstein had such a sad face. But the *acts* he had. The big time. He had Eva Tanguay. Willie Howard. Acts like that."

We passed shooting galleries, hot-dog stands, and theatres showing movies like "Outcast Girls" and "Female Tricks of the Trade."

"There used to be a white tile Child's restaurant around about here," he said. "That Child's was wonderful. It was all *very* white. They used to make hotcakes right in their window. Forty-second Street was *very* elegant then. *Very* elegant. Belasco had a play, 'The Governor's Lady,' with Emma Dunn, in which he reproduced a Child's—every detail. Belasco believed in being very realistic. What a meal you could get at Child's for a quarter, plus dessert! Or two eggs, hot biscuits, and wonderful hot coffee, all for fifteen cents."

Chaplin walked up to Forty-third Street and over to Eighth Avenue, past Andy's Food Shop, the Times Grill, the Dixie Bus Depot, and the Hotel Times Square, and back down to Forty-second.

"The American Music Hall used to have two theatres in it," he said. "You'd take an elevator and go up and play to another audience. Don't tell me there's a bank there now. That would be horrifying. No, the Anco Theatre. That's it. 'The Thrill Film Theatre, Robin Hood—The Half Breed,' " he read from the marquee. "My God! How the whole place gets lost, doesn't it? Let's go up to the next corner. I'm a little cloudy about this, but I know the Eltinge Theatre was around here, too. Julian Eltinge was a great vaudeville star. A female impersonator."

An old woman in a torn dress was standing in front of the New Amsterdam Theatre selling pretzels from a battered baby stroller. "I don't think the old girl would know whether this is where Ziegfeld had his 'Follies,' or whether it had a roof garden," Chaplin said. He stopped walking. He looked puzzled, a bit hurt.

An elderly man with a pale, freckled face, who was bald except for reddish hair at the base of his skull, came along and stopped beside us. He wore a dirty white shirt open at the collar, and he had a bundle of old newspapers under one arm. "Visiting your old haunts, Charlie?" he said to Chaplin.

"Why, yes," Chaplin said. "Yes. Yes, I am."

"I used to come in as a kid, fifteen years old," the man said. "I used to see you. They were good old days."

"Wasn't this where Ziegfeld had his 'Follies'?" Chaplin asked. "And didn't it have a roof garden upstairs?"

"You're right," the man said. "And it still does have a roof garden."

"You see, I was right, wasn't I?" Chaplin said to me.

"What are you doing now, Charlie?" the man asked.

"I'm still in the movies," Chaplin said. "At least, I *think* I am." He gave his laugh.

Chaplin spent the last quarter-century of his life in Corsier-sur-Vevey, Switzerland, a twenty-minute drive from Lausanne. He lived, with his family, in a beautiful old manor house—Le Manoir de Ban—on thirty-seven acres of vast lawns, ancient pine trees, and orchards, where he had a swimming pool and a tennis court and also a view of Lake Geneva and the Alps. There he and Oona had four more children—Eugene, Jane, Annette, and Christopher. They made their home an open one to their friends. The Chaplins relished hearing about life back in the United States, but they evidently had no longing for it. A few months after they had moved into their new home, I visited them. Chaplin and Oona were visibly happy with each other, with their children, and with their surroundings. "We couldn't have found a more nearly perfect place to live," Chaplin told me. "The kids can go to the best schools in the world right here. They've already learned to speak French. And if Oona and I get bored, we can pop over to London or to Paris in an hour or two."

From what I saw, the Swiss enjoyed having Chaplin among them. Whenever he walked or drove (he owned a black Ford sedan and liked to drive it) on the streets, he was recognized more often than he had been on Fifth Avenue before he left, but the recognition was always limited to a cheerful shout of *"Bonjour, Charlot!"*

The Chaplins ate outdoors as often as possible, on a large terrace overlooking a long expanse of lawn, and the mountains in the distance. Wild strawberries with heavy cream provided an occasion for a kind of dramatic production by Chaplin. He would choose the best-looking ones and present

36

them, one at a time, to Oona, to himself, to a guest, and to each of his children—in that order. He would eat them with exaggerated appreciation. At the close of one such production, he shared a confidence with me. "Every once in a while," he said, "the old lady and I get out the caviar and champagne. And we don't invite anybody else. We sit here gorging ourselves. Just the two of us."

One night toward the end of their first year in Switzerland, the Chaplins invited me to accompany them and Geraldine, then nine, and Josephine, then four, to a Swiss circus, the Knie, playing near Lausanne. The circus was owned by the Knie brothers, Rolf and Fredy, and the performers included other members of the Knie family; a famous wire-walker, Reco, who always dressed as a clown; and Lippizaners, lions, tigers, and ten dancing elephants. One of the dancing elephants wore oversized Chaplin shoes and an undersized Chaplin coat, had a derby on his head, and carried a cane in his trunk. After he had danced, the crowd cheered, and there were calls for "Charlot! Charlot!" from people who had noticed Chaplin in the audience. Rolf Knie, a rather portly gentleman, who was the elephant trainer, held out a large loaf of bread to Chaplin and invited him to come into the ring. Shyly, Chaplin, who was wearing a dark-blue pin-striped business suit, got up, entered the ring, took the bread in his left hand, and deferentially offered it to the derby-wearing elephant. The elephant accepted it, and bowed to Chaplin, who bowed back. The audience cheered as Chaplin returned to his seat.

After the circus ended, the Knie brothers invited Chaplin and the rest of us into their home, a trailer parked near the circus tent. We all gathered around a small table in the trailer with the brothers and their wives and with Reco, the clown

Jerry Epstein, Lillian Ross, and Chaplin

Chaplin with Jerry Epstein, editing "Limelight"

Le Manoir de Ban, Corsier-sur-Vevey

Chaplin in Corsier-sur-Vevey

wire-walker. Mrs. Knie, the mother of Rolf and Fredy, loaded the table with ham sandwiches and beer.

"I saw every one of your films," Reco told Chaplin, in English. "When I was a kid, I used to steal bottles to get pennies to see your films. Do you remember the circus one? The way the monkeys got on the clown and he was trying to brush them off?"

"Yes, yes," Chaplin said. "And he can't get them off." He gave us a quick enactment of his own enactment of the scene. (I never heard Chaplin talk about any of his own characters in any person except the third or in any tense except the present.)

"And the one where you're making doughnuts and you're putting dynamite in the dough?" Rolf Knie said. "Do you remember that one?"

"Yes, yes," Chaplin said, laughing.

For the next two and a half hours, Chaplin sat with the circus people, talking about his movies for a while but rather quickly getting into reminiscences of famous London pantomimes, like "Cinderella" and "Puss in Boots." Then they all talked about old vaudeville people, and old vaudeville bits of business, like "taking the nap" (pretending to be hit), and after that they told circus stories—about tigers, about elephants, about horses. "I don't care for horses," Chaplin confided to them. He did a quick imitation of a horse, pawing at the ground.

After the stories about circus animals, they told stories about circus people, including dwarfs. Then there was a brief silence.

"Dwarfs are the hardest-working ones," Chaplin said. "They're very sad."

The Knies agreed.

"Circus is in the blood," Reco said. "In my family, being

in the circus goes back for generations. That is the way it goes."

"Oh, yes, yes," Chaplin said. "My father and mother both were in vaudeville, and also my aunt. When I was a small boy, I remember waiting up for my mother at night with my older brother, Syd. I was four years younger than Syd. My mother in her act wore a cap and gown, recited a verse, and did a dance. She was one of the first champions of women's rights, by the way. We'd wait up, and she'd usually bring us a Napoleon slice or some other sweet and tell us how it went that night."

Geraldine and Josephine, who had been sitting by quietly, eating ham sandwiches, were nodding off, and Rolf Knie noticed them.

"I have children, but no girls," Rolf Knie, who looked somewhat like an elephant himself, said wistfully.

"My mother had only boys," Chaplin said. "At first, I had only boys, and suddenly I had girls. I like them. They decorate the house." He looked at Josephine, who looked back at him with sleepily blinking eyes. "That one looks just like Mabel Normand," he said to the Knies. "Remember her?"

"Mabel Normand, certainly—in the Keystone comedies!" one of the Knie brothers said enthusiastically.

"Sweet Mabel," Chaplin said, and he gave a little laugh.

The Chaplins had their eighth, and last, child—Christopher —in 1962. A visit to Le Manoir de Ban invariably started with greetings from beautiful small pigtailed girls, who had enormous round eyes, and who would be wearing handmade white Swiss-cotton dresses that had been worn a few years earlier by their elder sisters. Or, at dinner, these children, along with a quiet boy or two, would sit, at the foot of the long table, bathed and immaculate and wearing white fleecy robes and slippers. A few giggles. A mild complaint. One or

Chaplin with Josephine and Geraldine at
a performance of Grock, the clown

Chaplin with Annette

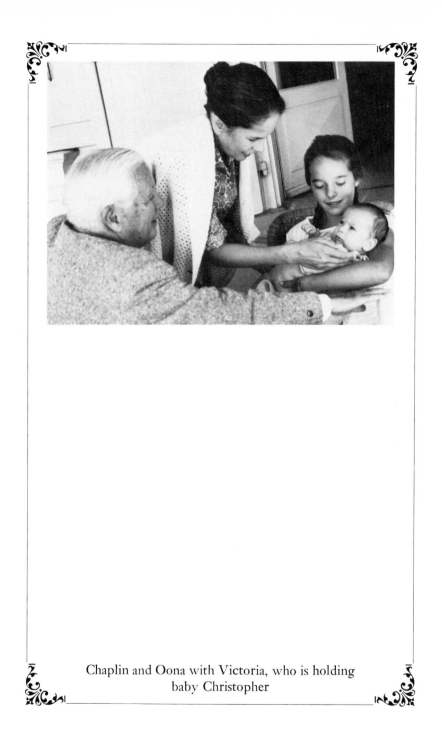

Chaplin and Oona with Victoria, who is holding
baby Christopher

Chaplin with Josephine

two nicely modulated, brief argumentative remarks, such as Josephine (at the age of ten) saying to Victoria (at eight), "My French is Frencher than yours." But minding their manners, deferring to the elders, and departing without protest to their upstairs quarters as soon as they had eaten. Some of the moments I remember from Vevey had the atmosphere of something staged, real though they were:

Charlie Chaplin heading for his tennis court, wearing white flannel trousers and a tennis shirt with a collar—a white cable-knit sweater dashingly slung over his back, the sleeves tied in front.

Charlie Chaplin playing tennis, racquet in his left hand, running for every ball, not liking to lose, and showing his dissatisfaction every time he lost a point, giving his all to the game, in total concentration, and never, *never* losing track of the score.

Charlie Chaplin obliging—before or after meals at home, before or after meals in restaurants—his children, his wife, and his friends by doing the famous "dance of the dinner rolls" just as he did it, with forks stuck in the rolls to make them look like feet, in "The Gold Rush."

Charlie Chaplin sharing a bowl of peanuts with three-year-old Annette. Chaplin's face would be down over the bowl, and he would be glaring, in top performance, leaving no doubt as to who would get the last peanut.

Charlie Chaplin in a long white terry-cloth robe, his pure-white hair dishevelled, leading a visitor at eight o'clock on a late-summer morning down his lawn to his swimming pool, all the whites looking whiter in contrast to the shadows cast by the trees on the smooth green lawn.

Charlie Chaplin at the pool, saying, "I go up and down the pool once and then out. I keep the water warm. It's not easy to go from a warm bed into a cold pool. I like it as long as I'm warm."

Charlie Chaplin sitting in front of a big fire in the fireplace of his living room for a quick drink before dinner. Gin-and-tonic, usually. "I look forward to that one drink at night," he would say. (One evening, the doors to the living room had been left ajar, and sounds came in of a man singing, in French, on a record being played somewhere in the recesses of the big house:

> *Banjo Boy, Banjo Boy,*
> *Qui s'en va,*
> *Les pieds nus,*
> *Tout le long des rues*
> *En chan-tant*
> *A pleine voix.*
> *Banjo Boy, Banjo Boy.*

"All the kids speak French now as well as English, you know, but not me," Chaplin said to me, pretending to frown at the song. "It's rather nice, you know, *not* to speak the language of the country you're in.")

Charlie Chaplin after dinner, showing home movies, or some of his old pictures, to anybody who happened to be in his house, fussing over the projector himself, keeping up a running commentary on whatever he was showing, and acting out most of the parts himself.

Charlie Chaplin comforting Victoria, at the age of eleven, after she had seen "Limelight" for the first time. ("I couldn't help crying at the end, when you died," Victoria said to her father. "Oh, my dear," Chaplin said, on the verge of tears himself. "Oh, my dear. That's sweet. So sweet.")

Charlie Chaplin making a confession about the origins of "The Great Dictator": "When I first saw Hitler, with that little mustache, I thought he was copying *me*, taking advantage of my success. I was that egotistical."

Charlie Chaplin at the piano in his living room, playing music he had composed for his pictures, humming along with his own playing, while his face expressed every emotion experienced by everybody in each picture, and simultaneously talking: "I can't play anybody's music but my own. I never took a lesson. I never even *saw* a piano close up until I was twenty-one. As soon as I touched the piano, I could play. The same with the violin."

Charlie Chaplin, at five o'clock in the morning, heading quietly for his study, to work alone on his autobiography, as he did every morning for several years. (In 1962, on an afternoon in early September, I sat with him on his terrace as he read parts of his book manuscript to me, the tortoiseshell-rimmed glasses a bit down on his nose, his reading dramatic to the point of melodrama, his devotion to his subject unself-conscious and complete. "I use Fowler's 'The King's English' as my guide," he told me during a breather. "I do all my own editing. I'm very particular. I like to see a clean page, with no erasures. I'm entirely self-taught.")

Chaplin loved to sit around with his friends and talk about how he happened to invent bits of business in his movies. He always reënacted his bits of business as he told about them. To be anywhere with him invariably meant watching him either do a forever-fresh old bit of business or invent a new bit of business for the fun of it. He never stopped inventing.

After moving to Switzerland, he continued to enjoy playing the guide on walking tours—in Lausanne, in Geneva, or in Vevey, the village near his home, in which he liked to point out where Byron and Shelley had lived, had worked, had eaten. "You must see the little village of Saint-Saphorin, with those beautiful little crooked streets,"

Jerry Epstein directing Chaplin's son Sydney in the
movie "My Son, the Imposter"

Geraldine Chaplin

Victoria Chaplin and her husband,
Jean-Baptiste Thierrée, in costume for their circus,
Le Cirque Imaginaire

Michael and Josephine

Oona, Victoria, and Victoria's son,
James-Baptiste Thierrée

Chaplin reading aloud from manuscript
of his autobiography

The Chaplins' Christmas card, 1964.
Back, left to right: Annette, Jane, Eugene, Victoria, Josephine.
Front, left to right: Christopher, Oona, Chaplin

Chaplin coming from seats into ring with elephant
at the Knie Circus

Chaplin kidding around on the lawn
at home in Corsier

Chaplin inventing "a bit of business"

he once said to me and to Jerry Epstein, who was also visiting the Chaplins. "It's so sweet. As a matter of fact, let's go there right now." He drove us there in his Ford sedan, parked the car, and led us up one of the narrowest of the crooked streets. At one point, he got a bit ahead of Jerry Epstein and me. While he was waiting for us to catch up, he suddenly invented a bit of business—he leaned against an old building, crossed his legs, put his hands in his trouser pockets, and hunched over, glaring at us laggards.

Other bits of business:

Charlie Chaplin, barefoot, is on his way back to the house from a swim in the pool, a small white terry-cloth towel wrapped around his middle. A visitor appears on the terrace. Chaplin curls his forefingers alongside the ends of his eyebrows and raises a prancing leg, like Pan.

Charlie Chaplin gets his hands on one of his children's balloons and immediately kicks it backward to the child, just as he did with the balloon of the world in "The Great Dictator," and then laughs at the squeals of approval from his small audience.

The Chaplins were faithful with their Christmas cards, which always included a conventional family photograph of one kind or another, usually taken in their living room or on the lawn in front of their house. The children would be lined up in order of age. In the photographs, Chaplin didn't kid around; he always looked strictly the head of the family. There is just a hint of a departure from that role in the Christmas photograph taken in 1964, the year "My Autobiography" was published. It shows the clan reading the book, three members holding copies of the British edition and each of the others holding an edition published in a different country. (Two-year-old Christopher, bare-legged, with white socks and black patent leather shoes, has "Chaplin: Mit Liv.") Chaplin in this photograph wears an expression of fake, overdone concentration. The next year, the family is shown standing ankle-deep in snow, with everybody wearing a parka and ski pants—everybody except Chaplin himself, who has on a dark double-breasted overcoat, a dark suit, a white shirt, a dark necktie, and a black fedora. He is standing straight, head up, grinning proudly, hands in his overcoat pockets. The 1968 card bears the inscription, in Oona's handwriting, "25th Wedding Anniversary," and it shows the family gathered on and around the livingroom sofa, everybody, including Chaplin, looking self-conscious, giving the obligatory anniversary smile. The photograph for Christmas, 1976, shows Chaplin and Oona seated in a golf cart, useful for getting around large lawns, and surrounded by their children and, by then, grandchildren.

The Christmas card for 1977 arrived just before Christmas Day, which was the day Charlie Chaplin died. The photograph is of Charlie Chaplin alone, and was taken on April 16, 1977, his last birthday—his eighty-eighth. He is sitting in a chair and is wearing a dark suit over a baby-blue cashmere sweater. The white collar of his shirt comes down over the sweater, and there is a white handkerchief in the breast pocket of his jacket. His white hair is sparser but still full and is combed neatly from a side part. His right hand is holding a walking stick. His left hand is raised—a bit of the blue sweater showing at the wrist—and is held in midair to a position over his heart, in the classic gesture of the actor.

The Chaplins' last Christmas card, 1977